365 Motivatio

The following 365 are a combination of motivational quotes that you can use better yourself and your mindset and set yourself up for massive amounts of Empower Encourage Happiness Success Motivation in your life

You should hopefully have a good understanding of how to utilize affirmation for the best result. You can pick and choose which of these you like the most, but try not to quickly read through all of these ones after another, unless that is how you like to do it and works best for you.

Change Your Life Today With Some of the Greatest Book of 365 Motivational Quotes to Give You the Kickstart You Need!

Motivational Quotes

1

"I must not fear. Fear is the mind-killer. Fear is the little-death that brings total obliteration. I will face my fear. I will permit it to pass over me and through me. And when it has gone past I will turn the inner eye to see its path. Where the fear has gone there will be nothing. Only I will remain."
— Frank Herbert, Dune

2

"The truth is, unless you let go, unless you forgive yourself, unless you forgive the situation, unless you realize that the situation is over, you cannot move forward."
— Steve Maraboli

3

"Letting go means to come to the realization that some people are a part of your history, but not a part of your destiny."
— Steve Maraboli

4

"Lack of direction, not lack of time, is the problem. We all have twenty-four hour days."
— Zig Ziglar

5

"Cry. Forgive. Learn. Move on. Let your tears water the seeds of your future happiness."
— Steve Maraboli

6

"Incredible change happens in your life when you decide to take control of what you do have power over instead of craving control over what you don't."
— Steve Maraboli

7

"Everything can be taken from a man but one thing: the last of the human freedoms—to choose one's attitude in any given set of circumstances, to choose one's own way."
— Viktor E. Frankl

8

"The only way of discovering the limits of the possible is to venture a little way past them into the impossible."
— Arthur C. Clarke

9

"Sometimes life knocks you on your ass... get up, get up, get up!!! Happiness is not the absence of problems, it's the ability to deal with them."
— Steve Maraboli

Motivational Quotes

10

"The man who moves a mountain begins by carrying away small stones."
— Confucius

11

"Happiness is not the absence of problems, it's the ability to deal with them."
— Steve Maraboli

12

"Without ambition one starts nothing. Without work one finishes nothing. The prize will not be sent to you. You have to win it."
— Ralph Waldo Emerson

13

"Change the way you look at things and the things you look at change."
— Wayne W. Dyer

14

"When in a relationship, a real man doesn't make his woman jealous of others, he makes others jealous of his woman."
— Steve Maraboli

15

"Circumstances are the rulers of the weak; they are but the instruments of the wise."
— Samuel Lover

16

"We all make mistakes, have struggles, and even regret things in our past. But you are not your mistakes, you are not your struggles, and you are here NOW with the power to shape your day and your future."
— Steve Maraboli

17

"At the end of the day, let there be no excuses, no explanations, no regrets."
— Steve Maraboli

18

"You must learn to let go. Release the stress. You were never in control anyway."
— Steve Maraboli

19

"Although the world is full of suffering, it is
full also of the overcoming of it."
— Helen Keller

20

"Learn the rules like a pro, so you can break
them like an artist."
— Pablo Picasso

21

"Make a pact with yourself today to not be
defined by your past. Sometimes the greatest
thing to come out of all your hard work isn't
what you get for it, but what you become for
it. Shake things up today! Be You...Be
Free...Share."
— Steve Maraboli

Motivational Quotes

22

"It's only after you've stepped outside your
comfort zone that you begin to change,
grow, and transform."
— Roy T. Bennett

23

"I will not try to convince you to love me, to
respect me, to commit to me. I deserve better
than that; I AM BETTER THAN
THAT...Goodbye."
— Steve Maraboli

24

"Do not stop thinking of life as an adventure.
You have no security unless you can live
bravely, excitingly, imaginatively; unless
you can choose a challenge instead of
competence."
— Eleanor Roosevelt

Motivational Quotes

25

"Attitude is a choice. Happiness is a choice. Optimism is a choice. Kindness is a choice. Giving is a choice. Respect is a choice. Whatever choice you make makes you. Choose wisely."
— Roy T. Bennett

26

"If you hang out with chickens, you're going to cluck and if you hang out with eagles, you're going to fly."
— Steve Maraboli, Unapologetically You: Reflections on Life and the Human Experience

27

"How would your life be different if…You walked away from gossip and verbal defamation? Let today be the day…You speak only the good you know of other people and encourage others to do the same."
— Steve Maraboli

28

"Live the Life of Your Dreams: Be brave enough to live the life of your dreams according to your vision and purpose instead of the expectations and opinions of others."
— Roy T. Bennett

29

"Whatever the mind can conceive and believe, it can achieve."
— Napoleon Hill

30

"Renew, release, let go. Yesterday's gone. There's nothing you can do to bring it back. You can't "should've" done something. You can only DO something. Renew yourself. Release that attachment. Today is a new day!"
— Steve Maraboli

31

"People are always blaming their circumstances for what they are. I don't believe in circumstances. The people who get on in this world are the people who get up and look for the circumstances they want, and if they can't find them, make them."
— George Bernard Shaw

32

"Action may not always bring happiness, but there is no happiness without action. "
— William James

33

"Forget yesterday - it has already forgotten you. Don't sweat tomorrow - you haven't even met. Instead, open your eyes and your heart to a truly precious gift - today."
— Steve Maraboli,

Motivational Quotes

34

"You have to accept whatever comes, and the only important thing is that you meet it with the best you have to give."
— Eleanor Roosevelt

35

"I write for the same reason I breathe - because if I didn't, I would die."
— Isaac Asimov

36

"Only he who attempts the absurd is capable of achieving the impossible."
— Miguel de Unamuno

37

"In the end, you have to choose whether or not to trust someone."
— Sophie Kinsella

38

"You are the average of the five people you spend the most time with."
— Jim Rohn

39

"You never change your life until you step out of your comfort zone; change begins at the end of your comfort zone."
— Roy T. Bennett

Motivational Quotes

40

"Don't be pushed around by the fears in your mind. Be led by the dreams in your heart."
— Roy T. Bennett

41

"Be grateful for what you already have while you pursue your goals.
If you aren't grateful for what you already have, what makes you think you would be happy with more."
— Roy T. Bennett

42

"Stop giving other people the power to control your happiness, your mind, and your life. If you don't take control of yourself and your own life, someone else is bound to try."
— Roy T. Bennett

Motivational Quotes

43

"Always remember people who have helped you along the way, and don't forget to lift someone up."
— Roy T. Bennett

44

"Let the improvement of yourself keep you so busy that you have no time to criticize others."
— Roy T. Bennett

45

"Do not let the memories of your past limit the potential of your future. There are no limits to what you can achieve on your journey through life, except in your mind."
— Roy T. Bennett

Motivational Quotes

46

"When the going gets tough, put one foot in front of the other and just keep going. Don't give up."
— Roy T. Bennett

47

"How would your life be different if…You stopped allowing other people to dilute or poison your day with their words or opinions? Let today be the day…You stand strong in the truth of your beauty and journey through your day without attachment to the validation of others"
— Steve Maraboli

48

"I want to live my life in such a way that when I get out of bed in the morning, the devil says, "aw shit, he's up!"
— Steve Maraboli

49

"When the going gets tough, put one foot in front of the other and just keep going. Don't give up."
— Roy T. Bennett

50

"How would your life be different if…You stopped allowing other people to dilute or poison your day with their words or opinions? Let today be the day…You stand strong in the truth of your beauty and journey through your day without attachment to the validation of others"
— Steve Maraboli

51

"I want to live my life in such a way that when I get out of bed in the morning, the devil says, "aw shit, he's up!"
— Steve Maraboli

Motivational Quotes

52

"Surround Yourself with People Who Believe in Your Dreams:
Surround yourself with people who believe in your dreams, encourage your ideas, support your ambitions, and bring out the best in you."
— Roy T. Bennett

53

"Success is not how high you have climbed, but how you make a positive difference to the world."
— Roy T. Bennett

54

"Life is about accepting the challenges along the way, choosing to keep moving forward, and savoring the journey."
— Roy T. Bennett

55

"Maturity is when you stop complaining and making excuses, and start making changes."
— Roy T. Bennett

56

"Don't wish it were easier. Wish you were better."
— Jim Rohn

57

"Don't confuse poor decision-making with destiny. Own your mistakes. It's ok; we all make them. Learn from them so they can empower you!"
— Steve Maraboli

58

"You Are the Master of Your Attitude

You cannot control what happens to you, but you can control the way you think about all the events. You always have a choice. You can choose to face them with a positive mental attitude."
— Roy T. Bennett

59

"It doesn't matter what you did or where you were...it matters where you are and what you're doing. Get out there! Sing the song in your heart and NEVER let anyone shut you up!!"
— Steve Maraboli

60

"I cannot let the fear of the past color the future."
— Julie Kagawa

61

"What's done is done. What's gone is gone. One of life's lessons is always moving on. It's okay to look back to see how far you've come but keep moving forward."
— Roy T. Bennett

62

"Once you realize you deserve a bright future, letting go of your dark past is the best choice you will ever make."
— Roy T. Bennett

63

"Let today be the day you stop being haunted by the ghost of yesterday. Holding a grudge & harboring anger/resentment is poison to the soul. Get even with people...but not those who have hurt us, forget them, instead get even with those who have helped us."
— Steve Maraboli

Motivational Quotes

64

"Courage is feeling fear, not getting rid of fear, and taking action in the face of fear."
— Roy T. Bennett

65

"Do what is right, not what is easy nor what is popular."
— Roy T. Bennett

66

"LAW 4
Always Say Less Than Necessary

When you are trying to impress people with words, the more you say, the more common you appear, and the less in control. Even if you are saying something banal, it will seem original if you make it vague, open-ended, and sphinxlike. Powerful people impress and intimidate by saying less. The more you say, the more likely you are to say something foolish."
— Robert Greene

67

"Don't fear failure. — Not failure, but low aim, is the crime. In great attempts it is glorious even to fail."
— Bruce Lee

68

"Pursue what catches your heart, not what catches your eyes."
— Roy T. Bennett

69

"One resolution I have made, and try always to keep, is this: 'To rise above little things'."
— John Burroughs

Motivational Quotes

70

"Believe in your infinite potential. Your only limitations are those you set upon yourself."
— Roy T. Bennett

71

"Time is an equal opportunity employer. Each human being has exactly the same number of hours and minutes every day. Rich people can't buy more hours. Scientists can't invent new minutes. And you can't save time to spend it on another day. Even so, time is amazingly fair and forgiving. No matter how much time you've wasted in the past, you still have an entire tomorrow."
— Denis Waitley

72

"Want to keep Christ in Christmas? Feed the hungry, clothe the naked, forgive the guilty, welcome the unwanted, care for the ill, love your enemies, and do unto others as you would have done unto you."
— Steve Maraboli,

Motivational Quotes

73

"If you have a strong purpose in life, you don't have to be pushed. Your passion will drive you there."
— Roy T. Bennett

74

"My past has not defined me, destroyed me, deterred me, or defeated me; it has only strengthened me."
— Steve Maraboli

75

"Never respond to an angry person with a fiery comeback, even if he deserves it...Don't allow his anger to become your anger."
— Bohdi Sanders

Motivational Quotes

76

"Plant seeds of happiness, hope, success, and love; it will all come back to you in abundance. This is the law of nature."
— Steve Maraboli

77

"Patience Is Not the Ability to Wait: Patience is not the ability to wait. Patience is to be calm no matter what happens, constantly take action to turn it to positive growth opportunities, and have faith to believe that it will all work out in the end while you are waiting."
— Roy T. Bennett

78

"Be silent and safe — silence never betrays you;
Be true to your word and your work and your friend;
Put least trust in him who is foremost to praise you,
Nor judge of a road till it draw to the end."
— John Boyle O'Reilly

Motivational Quotes

79

"You were put on this earth to achieve your greatest self, to live out your purpose, and to do it courageously."
— Steve Maraboli

80

"It doesn't matter if a million people tell you what you can't do, or if ten million tell you no. If you get one yes from God that's all you need."
— Tyler Perry

81

"You are essentially who you create yourself to be and all that occurs in your life is the result of your own making."
— Stephen Richards

Motivational Quotes

82

"The universe doesn't give you what you ask
for with your thoughts - it gives you what
you demand with your actions."
— Steve Maraboli

83

"The reason many people in our society are
miserable, sick, and highly stressed is because
of an unhealthy attachment to things they
have no control over."
— Steve Maraboli

84

"Be brave to stand for what you believe in
even if you stand alone."
— Roy T. Bennett

85

"Dreams don't work unless you take action. The surest way to make your dreams come true is to live them."
— Roy T. Bennett

86

"Challenge and adversity are meant to help you know who you are. Storms hit your weakness, but unlock your true strength."
— Roy T. Bennett

87

"Strong people have a strong sense of self-worth and self-awareness; they don't need the approval of others."
— Roy T. Bennett

88

"It takes sunshine and rain to make a rainbow. There would be no rainbows without sunshine and rain."
— Roy T. Bennett

89

"You are not a victim. No matter what you have been through, you're still here. You may have been challenged, hurt, betrayed, beaten, and discouraged, but nothing has defeated you. You are still here! You have been delayed but not denied. You are not a victim, you are a victor. You have a history of victory."
— Steve Maraboli,

90

"You cannot change anyone, but you can be the reason someone changes."
— Roy T. Bennett

91

"To have what you have never had, you have to do what you have never done."
— Roy T. Bennett

92

"Great leaders can see the greatness in others when they can't see it themselves and lead them to their highest potential they don't even know."
— Roy T. Bennett

93

"The strongest people find the courage and caring to help others, even if they are going through their own storm."
— Roy T. Bennett

Motivational Quotes

94

"If you believe very strongly in something, stand up and fight for it."
— Roy T. Bennett

95

"How would your life be different if…You stopped worrying about things you can't control and started focusing on the things you can? Let today be the day…You free yourself from fruitless worry, seize the day and take effective action on things you can change."
— Steve Maraboli

96

"The strongest people find the courage and caring to help others, even if they are going through "The comfort zone is a psychological state in which one feels familiar, safe, at ease, and secure. You never change your life until you step out of your comfort zone; change begins at the end of your comfort zone."
— Roy T. Bennetttheir own storm."
— Roy T. Bennett

Motivational Quotes

97

"The greatest step towards a life of simplicity is to learn to let go."
— Steve Maraboli,

98

"Do not let arrogance go to your head and despair to your heart; do not let compliments go to your head and criticisms to your heart; do not let success go to your head and failure to your heart."
— Roy T. Bennett

99

"Rejection is an opportunity for your selection."
— Bernard Branson

Motivational Quotes

100

"First say to yourself what you would be;
and then do what you have to do."
— Epictetus

101

"Keep in mind that the true measure of an
individual is how he treats a person who can
do him absolutely no good."
— Ann Landers

102

"Don't let others tell you what you can't do.
Don't let the limitations of others limit your
vision. If you can remove your self-doubt and
believe in yourself, you can achieve what
you never thought possible."
— Roy T. Bennett

103

"7 Effective Ways to Make Others Feel Important

1. Use their name.
2. Express sincere gratitude.
3. Do more listening than talking.
4. Talk more about them than about you.
5. Be authentically interested.
6. Be sincere in your praise.
7. Show you care."
— Roy T. Bennett

104

"Just an observation: it is impossible to be both grateful and depressed. Those with a grateful mindset tend to see the message in the mess. And even though life may knock them down, the grateful find reasons, if even small ones, to get up."
— Steve Maraboli

105

"Great leaders create more leaders, not followers."
— Roy T. Bennett

106

"Live the Life of Your Dreams
When you start living the life of your dreams, there will always be obstacles, doubters, mistakes and setbacks along the way. But with hard work, perseverance and self-belief there is no limit to what you can achieve."
— Roy T. Bennett

107

"You learn something valuable from all of the significant events and people, but you never touch your true potential until you challenge yourself to go beyond imposed limitations."
— Roy T. Bennett

108

"What you stay focused on will grow."
— Roy T. Bennett

109

"The biggest wall you have to climb is the one you build in your mind: Never let your mind talk you out of your dreams, trick you into giving up. Never let your mind become the greatest obstacle to success. To get your mind on the right track, the rest will follow."
— Roy T. Bennett

110

"Start each day with a positive thought and a grateful heart."
— Roy T. Bennett

111

"One of the best ways to influence people is to make them feel important."
— Roy T. Bennett

Motivational Quotes

112

"Don't wait for things to happen. Make them happen."
— Roy T. Bennett

113

"It's never too late to change your life for the better. You don't have to take huge steps to change your life. Making even the smallest changes to your daily routine can make a big difference to your life."
— Roy T. Bennett

114

"LAW 25
Re-Create Yourself

Do not accept the roles that society foists on you. Re-create yourself by forging a new identity, one that commands attention and never bores the audience. Be the master of your own image rather than letting others define if for you. Incorporate dramatic devices into your public gestures and actions – your power will be enhanced and your character will seem larger than life."
— Robert Greene

115

"Free yourself from the complexities and drama of your life. Simplify. Look within. Within ourselves we all have the gifts and talents we need to fulfill the purpose we've been blessed with."
— Steve Maraboli

116

"I cannot compromise my respect for your love. You can keep your love, I will keep my respect."
— Amit Kalantri

117

"Everything is hard before it is easy"
— Johann Wolfgang von Goethe

118

"The harder you fall, the heavier your heart; the heavier your heart, the stronger you climb; the stronger you climb, the higher your pedestal."
— Criss Jami

119

"After sleeping through a hundred million centuries we have finally opened our eyes on a sumptuous planet, sparkling with color, bountiful with life. Within decades we must close our eyes again. Isn't it a noble, an enlightened way of spending our brief time in the sun, to work at understanding the universe and how we have come to wake up in it? This is how I answer when I am asked—as I am surprisingly often—why I bother to get up in the mornings."
— Richard Dawkins

120

"When things do not go your way, remember that every challenge — every adversity — contains within it the seeds of opportunity and growth."
— Roy T. Bennett

121

"Enthusiasm can help you find the new doors, but it takes passion to open them. If you have a strong purpose in life, you don't have to be pushed. Your passion will drive you there."
— Roy T. Bennett

122

"One must always be prepared for riotous and endless waves of transformation."
— Elizabeth Gilbert

123

"Great Leaders Create More Leaders

Good leaders have vision and inspire others to help them turn vision into reality. Great leaders create more leaders, not followers. Great leaders have vision, share vision, and inspire others to create their own."
— Roy T. Bennett

124

"One must always be prepared for riotous and endless waves of transformation."
— Elizabeth Gilbert

125

"Consistency is the true foundation of trust. Either keep your promises or do not make them."
— Roy T. Bennett

126

"Difficulties and adversities viciously force all their might on us and cause us to fall apart, but they are necessary elements of individual growth and reveal our true potential. We have got to endure and overcome them, and move forward. Never lose hope. Storms make people stronger and never last forever."
— Roy T. Bennett

127

"Your complaints, your drama, your victim mentality, your whining, your blaming, and all of your excuses have NEVER gotten you even a single step closer to your goals or dreams. Let go of your nonsense. Let go of the delusion that you DESERVE better and go EARN it! Today is a new day!"
— Steve Maraboli

128

"If you believe you can, you might. If you know you can, you will."
— Steve Maraboli

129

"It is impossible to discourage the real writers - they don't give a damn what you say, they're going to write."
— Sinclair Lewis

Motivational Quotes

130

"The discontent and frustration that you feel is entirely your own creation."
— Stephen Richards

131

"Live boldly. Push yourself. Don't settle."
— Jojo Moyes

132

"Never stop dreaming,
never stop believing,
never give up,
never stop trying, and
never stop learning."
— Roy T. Bennett

133

"Each day brings new opportunities, allowing you to constantly live with love—be there for others—bring a little light into someone's day. Be grateful and live each day to the fullest."
— Roy T. Bennett

134

"Never lose hope. Storms make people stronger and never last forever."
— Roy T. Bennett,

135

"Do what you love, love what you do, and with all your heart give yourself to it."
— Roy T. Bennett,

136

"Sometimes it's worth lingering on the journey for a while before getting to the destination."
— Richelle Mead

137

"LAW 38
Think As You Like But Behave Like Others
If you make a show of going against the times, flaunting your unconventional ideas and unorthodox ways, people will think that you only want attention and that you look down upon them. They will find a way to punish you for making them feel inferior. It is far safer to blend in and nurture the common touch. Share your originality only with tolerant friends and those who are sure to appreciate your uniqueness."
— Robert Greene

138

"Change may not always bring growth, but there is no growth without change."
— Roy T. Bennett

139

"If you don't give up on something you truly believe in, you will find a way."
— Roy T. Bennett

140

"When you concentrate your energy purposely on the future possibility that you aspire to realize, your energy is passed on to it and makes it attracted to you with a force stronger than the one you directed towards it."
— Stephen Richards

141

"No matter how much experience you have, there's always something new you can learn and room for improvement."
— Roy T. Bennett

Motivational Quotes

142

"What the mind can conceive and believe,
and the heart desire, you can achieve."
— Norman Vincent Peale

143

"Faith moves mountains, love transforms
hearts."
— John Paul Warren

144

"Don't chase people. Be yourself, do your own
thing and work hard. The right people - the
ones who really belong in your life - will
come to your. And stay."
— Will Smith

145

"It's not what we do once in a while that shapes our lives. It's what we do consistently."
— Anthony Robbins

146

"A young outcast will often feel that there is something wrong with himself, but as he gets older, grows more confident in who he is, he will adapt, he will begin to feel that there is something wrong with everyone else."
— Criss Jami, Killosophy

147

"We have been called to heal wounds, to unite what has fallen apart, and to bring home those who have lost their way."
— Francis of Assisi

148

"Do what you think is right. Don't let people make the decision of right or wrong for you."
— Steve Maraboli

149

"Remember to look up at the stars and not down at your feet. Try to make sense of what you see and wonder about what makes the universe exist. Be curious. And however difficult life may seem, there is always something you can do and succeed at.
It matters that you don't just give up."
— Stephen Hawking

150

"You are never alone. You are eternally connected with everyone."
— Amit Ray

151

"God helps those who strut their stuff."
— Dan Sofer

152

"Today is a new day. It's a day you have never seen before and will never see again. Stop telling yourself the 'same crap, different day' lie! How many days has that lie stolen from you? Seize the wonder and uniqueness of today! Recognize that throughout this beautiful day, you have an incredible amount of opportunities to move your life into the direction you want it to go."
— Steve Maraboli

153

"Holding a grudge & harboring anger/resentment is poison to the soul. Get even with people...but not those who have hurt us, forget them, instead get even with those who have helped us."
— Steve Maraboli

Motivational Quotes

154

"God is whispering in your heart, in the whole existence, just tune your ears."
— Amit Ray

155

"Act the way you'd like to be and soon you'll be the way you'd like to act."
— Bob Dylan

156

"Let go of something old that no longer serves you in order to make room for something new."
— Roy T. Bennett

157

"To be heroic is to be courageous enough to die for something; to be inspirational is to be crazy enough to live a little."
— Criss Jami

158

"Be careful the stories you're telling yourself about your current circumstances; a head full of negative thoughts has no space for positive ones."
— Roy T. Bennett

159

"Love is as simple as the absence of self given to another. God, when invited, fills the void of any unrequited love; hence loving is how one is drawn closer to God no matter its most horrific repercussions."
— Criss Jami

160

"Make your work to be in keeping with your
purpose"
— Leonardo da Vinci

161

"People will always have opinions about your
decision because they're not courageous
enough to take action on their opinion."
— Steve Maraboli

162

"Don't give up! It's not over. The universe is
balanced. Every set-back bears with it the
seeds of a come-back."
— Steve Maraboli, Unapologetically You:
Reflections on Life and the Human
Experience

163

"The spirit of the individual is determined by his dominating thought habits."
— Bruce Lee

164

"Our deepest fear is not that we are inadequate. Our deepest fear is that we are powerful beyond measure. It is our light, not our darkness that most frightens us. We ask ourselves, Who am I to be brilliant, gorgeous, talented, fabulous? Actually, who are you not to be?"
— Marianne Williamson,

165

"I am not a victim. No matter what I have been through, I'm still here. I have a history of victory."
— Steve Maraboli

Motivational Quotes

166

"The most intriguing people you will encounter in this life are the people who had insights about you, that you didn't know about yourself."
— Shannon L. Alder

167

"Either you run the day or the day runs you.."
— Jim Rohn

168

"If you have a goal, write it down. If you do not write it down, you do not have a goal - you have a wish."
— Steve Maraboli,

169

"Find a purpose to serve, not a lifestyle to live."
— Criss Jami

170

"...yelling doesn't make a thing any more possible."
— Angie Sage

171

"Do not let another day go by where your dedication to other people's opinions is greater than your dedication to your own emotions!"
— Steve Maraboli

Motivational Quotes

172

"Accept yourself, your strengths, your weaknesses, your truths, and know what tools you have to fulfill your purpose."
— Steve Maraboli,

173

"When you take control of your attitude, you take control of your life."
— Roy T. Bennett

174

"Your greatest self has been waiting your whole life; don't make it wait any longer."
— Steve Maraboli,

Motivational Quotes

175

"Always Remember to take your Vitamins: Take your Vitamin A for ACTION, Vitamin B for Belief, Vitamin C for Confidence ,Vitamin D for Discipline, Vitamin E for Enthusiasm!!"
— Pablo

176

"Being defeated is often a temporary condition. Giving up is what makes it permanent."
— Marilyn Vos Savant

177

"You can't hang around waiting for somebody else to pull your strings. Destiny's what you make of it. You have to face whatever life throws at you. And if it throws more than you'd like, more than you think you can handle? Well then you just have to find the heroism within yourself and play out the hand you've been dealt. The universe never sets a challenge that can't be met. You just need to believe in yourself in order to find the strength to face it."
— Darren Shan,

178

"Simplify your life. You don't grow spiritual, you shrink spiritual."
— Steve Maraboli,

179

"People in general would rather die than forgive. It's that hard. If God said in plain language. "I'm giving you a choice, forgive or die," a lot of people would go ahead and order their coffin."
— Sue Monk Kidd

180

"Whether you know or not, you are the infinite potential of love, peace and joy"
— Amit Ray

Motivational Quotes

181

"Live life as though nobody is watching, and express yourself as though everyone is listening."
— Nelson Mandela

182

"Don't bother just to be better than your contemporaries or predecessors. Try to be better than yourself."
— William Faulkner

183

"Push yourself to do more and to experience more. Harness your energy to start expanding your dreams. Yes, expand your dreams. Don't accept a life of mediocrity when you hold such infinite potential within the fortress of your mind. Dare to tap into your greatness."
— Robin S. Sharma

Motivational Quotes

184

"Not all dreamers are winners, but all winners are dreamers. Your dream is the key to your future. The Bible says that, "without a vision (dream), a people perish." You need a dream, if you're going to succeed in anything you do."
— Mark Gorman

185

"My atheism, like that of Spinoza, is true piety towards the universe and denies only gods fashioned by men in their own image, to be servants of their human interests."
— George Santayana

186

"At school, new ideas are thrust at you every day. Out in the world, you'll have to find your inner motivation to seek for new ideas on your own."
— Bill Watterson

187

"Be with someone who inspires you and makes you be the best version of yourself."
— Roy T. Bennett

188

"The size of your dreams must always exceed your current capacity to achieve them. If your dreams do not scare you, they are not big enough."
— Ellen Johnson Sirleaf

189

"If you want to find happiness, find gratitude."
— Steve Maraboli

Motivational Quotes

190

"Orang yang tidak pernah dibakar panas mentari, mustahil menghargai rimbun berteduh - peribahasa Turki."
— Hasrizal Abdul Jamil

191

"Grateful souls focus on the happiness and abundance present in their lives and this in turn attracts more abundance and joy towards them."
— Stephen Richards,

192

"Never allow your mind to wander untamed like a wild animal that exists on the basis of survival of the fittest. Tame your mind with consistent focus on your goals and desires."
— Stephen Richards

193

"You are the perfect creation of God. Don't allow you to be down. God is experiencing through you."
— Amit Ray

194

"Make today worth remembering."
— Zig Ziglar

195

"Fear can only grow in darkness. Once you face fear with light, you win."
— Steve Maraboli

Motivational Quotes

196

"I hope you find true meaning, contentment, and passion in your life. I hope you navigate the difficult times and come out with greater strength and resolve. I hope you find whatever balance you seek with your eyes wide open. And I hope that you - yes, you - have the ambition to lean in to your career and run the world. Because the world needs you to change it."
— Sheryl Sandberg

197

"One of the best ways to influence people is to make those around you feel important."
— Roy T. Bennett

198

"Do it first and feel about it afterwards.' - Dagny Taggart"
— Ayn Rand

199

"You don't have to get it perfect, you just have to get it going. Babies don't walk the first time they try, but eventually they get it right"
— Jack Canfield

200

"To assess the quality of thoughts of people, don't listen to their words, but watch their actions."
— Amit Kalantri

201

"Annual income twenty pounds, annual expenditure nineteen six, result happiness. Annual income twenty pounds, annual expenditure twenty pound ought and six, result misery."
— Charles Dickens

Motivational Quotes

202

"When I face the desolate impossibility of writing five hundred pages, a sick sense of failure falls on me, and I know I can never do it. Then gradually, I write one page and then another. One day's work is all I can permit myself to contemplate."
— John Steinbeck

203

"Life itself is simple...it's just not easy."
— Steve Maraboli

204

"You know you're doing what you love when Sunday nights feel the same as Friday nights...."
— Donny Deutsch

205

"If an apology is followed by an excuse or a reason, it means they are going to commit same mistake again they just apologized for."
— Amit Kalantri

206

"Your agreement with reality defines your life."
— Steve Maraboli

207

"I may not be where I want to be but I'm thankful for not being where I used to be."
— Habeeb Akande

208

"The here and now is all we have, and if we play it right it's all we'll need."
— Ann Richards

209

"The moment you become friends with your inner Self, you realize that the failures or hindrances that you met earlier were caused more by your disconnected status with your inner Being."
— Stephen Richards,

210

"Soar with wit. Conquer with dignity. Handle with care."
— Criss Jami

211

"The whole value of solitude depends upon oneself; it may be a sanctuary or a prison, a haven of repose or a place of punishment, a heaven or a hell, as we ourselves make it."
— John Lubbock

212

"Everyone of us needs to show how much we care for each other and, in the process, care for ourselves."
— Diana Princess of Wales

213

"If you fuel your journey on the opinions of others, you are going to run out of gas."
— Steve Maraboli

Motivational Quotes

214

"Never say anything about yourself you don't want to come true"
— Brian Tracy

215

"We only live once. We all have an expiration date after that we will never come again. I am not saying that to make you sad. I am saying that so you can cherish each moment in your life and be grateful that you are here and you are Special"
— Pablo

216

"Make the most of the best and the least of the worst."
— Robert Louis Stevenson

Motivational Quotes

217

"Sometimes we forget about our own advantages because we focus on what we don't have. Just because you have to work a little harder at something that seems easier to others doesn't mean you're without your own talents."
— Chris Colfer

218

"A person doesn't have to change who he is to become better."
— Sidney Poitier,

219

"Success is a poor teacher"
— Robert T. Kiyosaki

Motivational Quotes

220

"Ever Tried. Ever Failed. No matter. Try again. Fail again. Fail better."
— Samuel Beckett

221

"I can't think of anything more disheartening than living a life without a clear purpose."
— Daniel Willey

222

"The difference between greed and ambition is a greedy person desires things he isn't prepared to work for."
— Habeeb Akande

223

"You can't learn in school what the world is going to do next year."
— Henry Ford

224

"What is the point of being on this Earth if you are going to be like everyone else?"
— Arnold Schwarzenegger

225

Interrupt your thoughts of "I should", with your action of doing."
— Steve Maraboli

Motivational Quotes

226

"Just because you're in a situation, doesn't
mean you have to be that situation. You're
not the situation you're in!"
— K.M. Johnson

227

"Your feelings wouldn't get hurt if you were
honest with yourself"
— Ty Gray

228

"I hear you say 'Why?' Always 'Why?' You
see things; and you say 'Why?' But I dream
things that never were; and I say 'Why not?"
— George Bernard Shaw

229

"It is not as much about who you used to be,
as it is about who you choose to be."
— Sanhita Baruah

230

"You can lose your MONEY. You can lose your
FRIENDS. You can lose your JOB and you can
lose your MARRIAGE...and still recover...as
long as there is HOPE. Never lose HOPE."
— John Paul Warren

231

"Persistence is to the character of man as
carbon is to steel."
— Napoleon Hill

232

"As with all other aspects of the narrative art, you will improve with practice, but practice will never make you perfect. Why should it? What fun would that be?"
— Stephen King

233

"Success can be defined in many ways but failure in only one ... quitting!"
— Gerard de Marigny

234

"If a man has his eyes bound, you can encourage him as much as you like to stare through the bandage, but he'll never see anything."
— Franz Kafka

Motivational Quotes

235

"I've learned that no matter how inspired, fired up and motivated you might be, the dark clouds will always set in"
— Bernard Kelvin Clive,

236

"There's only one thing that will make them stop hating you. And that's being so good at what you do that they can't ignore you."
— Orson Scott Card

237

"There is no tomorrow and there was no yesterday; if you truly want to accomplish your goals you must engulf yourself in today."
— Noel DeJesus

Motivational Quotes

238

"Too often we underestimate the power of a touch, a smile, a kind word, a listening ear, an honest accomplishment, or the smallest act of caring, all of which have the potential to turn a life around."
— Leo Buscaglia

239

"And worse I may be yet: the worst is not
So long as we can say 'This is the worst."
— William Shakespeare

240

"Write this down: My life is full of unlimited possibilities."
— Pablo

241

"It will be better to spent our energy on reality; the tangible facts, not thoughts of the past."
— Durgesh Satpathy

242

"Stop waiting for the right person to come into your life. Be the right person to come to someone's life"
— Leo Babauta

243

"If everyone is moving forward together, then success takes care of itself."
— Henry Ford

Motivational Quotes

244

"It will be better to spent our energy on reality; the tangible facts, not thoughts of the past."
— Durgesh Satpathy

245

"Stop waiting for the right person to come into your life. Be the right person to come to someone's life"
— Leo Babauta

246

"If everyone is moving forward together, then success takes care of itself."
— Henry Ford

247

"If it is bread that you seek, you will have
bread.
If it is the soul you seek, you will find the
soul.
If you understand this secret, you know you
are that which you seek."
— Jalaluddin Rumi

248

"Have you had a failure or rejection? You
could get bitter. That's one way to deal with it.
Or...you could just get BETTER. What do you
think?"
— Destiny Booze

249

"You don't have to be a hero to accomplish
great things---to compete. You can just be
an ordinary chap, sufficiently motivated to
reach challenging goals."
— Edmund Hillary

Motivational Quotes

250

"The lust for comfort kills the passions of the soul."
— Kahlil Gibran

251

"Leave your excuses and live your dreams!"
— Paul F. Davis

252

"The problem isn't that I think so highly of myself. It is just that you think so little of yourself. Live life BIG, BOLD and OUT LOUD!"
— Shannon L. Alder

Motivational Quotes

253

"It's not what you've got, it's what you use that makes a difference."
— Zig Ziglar

254

"You are where you are and what you are because of yourself, nothing else. Nature is neutral. Nature doesn't care. If you do what other successful people do, you will enjoy the same results and rewards that they do. And if you don't, you won't."
— Brian Tracy

255

"Life's a marathon, not a sprint."
— Phillip C. McGraw

Motivational Quotes

256

"What good has impatience ever brought? It has only served as the mother of mistakes and the father of irritation."
— Steve Maraboli

257

"I can't help you, I can only guide you, and you are the one who can help yourself."
— Durgesh Satpathy

258

"It is a profound and necessary truth that the deep things in science are not found because they are useful; they are found because it was possible to find them."
— J. Robert Oppenheimer

259

"Every challenge you encounter in life is a fork in the road. You have the choice to choose which way to go - backward, forward, breakdown or breakthrough."
— Ifeanyi Enoch Onuoha,

260

"There has never been a meaningful life built on easy street."
— John Paul Warren

261

"When the going gets tough, the tough get going"
— Billy Joel

Motivational Quotes

262

"But if we are talking in terms of making progress in life, we must understand that "good enough" is very different from "best."
— Paulo Coelho

263

"Your limits are somewhere up there, waiting for you to reach beyond infinity."
— Arnold Henry

264

"Prepare yourself for success. You have to see it coming to get there."
— Destiny Booze

265

"Where we fall are the stepping-stones for
our journey."
— Lolly Daskal

266

"You can only work on yourself. Start there."
— Alice O. Howell

267

"Let your action manifest your thought, your
belief and your passion."
— Mohammed Ali Bapir

Motivational Quotes

268

"What others think about you is none of your business."
— Jack Canfield

269

"Notice the difference between being in control and needing control."
— Marilyn Suttle

270

"I have realized that whatever good comes to me, comes from God, whatever bad comes to me, God has allowed it, and I choose to be thankful for both."
— Jeff Goins

Motivational Quotes

271

"Don't use yesterday's state of mind, to make today's decision."
— C. Nzingha Smith

272

"The future is greatly different than your life now, the actions that you take must also be greatly different. You cannot do the same thing and get something different."
— Steve Maraboli

273

"When someone who is suffering looks to you for compassion, it's indeed a blessing; you are chosen to be their Light in a moment of sorrow."
— Michelle Cruz-Rosado

Motivational Quotes

274

"Time waits for no one."
— Yasutaka Tsutsui

275

"There are two things essential if you want to enhance your Jedi self-confidence:

1/ belief that it is possible

2/ that self-help is the best help"
— Stephen Richards

276

"The face is the mirror of the mind, and eyes without speaking confess the secrets of the heart."
— Jerome

277

"Every great leader can take you back to a defining moment when they decided to lead"
— John Paul Warren

278

"Yet how hard most people work for mere dust and ashes and care, taking no thought of growing in knowledge and grace, never having time to get in sight of their own ignorance."
— John Muir

279

"Pursue your goal. Opinions be damned."
— Stacy Verdick Case

Motivational Quotes

280

"I must admit, that I have learned more from my negative experiences than I have ever learned from my positive one."
— John Paul Warren

281

"A real decision is measured by the fact that you've taken a new action. If there's no action, you haven't truly decided."
— Anthony Robbins

282

"Superhuman effort isn't worth a damn unless it achieves results."
— Ernest Shackleton

283

"Sometimes we have to soak ourselves in the tears and fears of the past to water our future gardens."
— Suzy Kassem

284

"Love is perhaps the only emotions that is boundless"
— Santosh Avvannavar

285

"Uncertainty will always be part of the taking charge process."
— Harold Geneen

286

"If the painter wishes to see beauties that charm him, it lies in his power to create them, and if he wishes to see monstrosities that are frightful, ridiculous, or truly pitiable, he is lord and God thereof."
— Leonardo da Vinci

287

"To be happy, you have to risk being unhappy."
— Ogwo David Emenike,

288

"The difference between those who adapted and those who didn't, Gorton said, was a willingness to totally commit."
— Arnold Schwarzenegger

289

"You will never get everything in life but you will get enough."
— Sanhita Baruah

290

"The power behind taking responsibility for your actions lies in putting an end to negative thought patterns. You no longer dwell on what went wrong or focus on whom you are going to blame. You don't waste time building roadblocks to your success. Instead, you are set free and can now focus on succeeding."
— Lorii Myers

291

"Believe with all your heart that you will do what you were made to do."
— Orison Swett Marden

292

"A mind of moderate capacity which closely pursues one study must infallibly arrive at great proficiency in that study."
— Mary Shelley

293

"Perseverance is the act of true role models and heroes."
— Liza M. Wiemer

294

"Once you figure out what you want in life —expect nothing less."
— Lorii Myers

295

"If you don't make the time to work on creating the life you want, you're eventually going to be forced to spend a LOT of time dealing with a life you don't want."
— Kevin Ngo

296

"The madder it makes you, the harder you need to laugh at it."
— Destiny Booze

297

"How many of us stop short of success on purpose? How many of us sabotage our own happiness because failure, while miserable, is a fear we're familiar with? Success, however, dreams come true, are a whole new kind of terrifying, an entire new species of responsibilities and disillusions, requiring a new way to think, act and become. Why do we REALLY quit? Because it's hopeless? Or because it's possible..."
— Jennifer DeLucy

298

"When something poses as obstacle to you,surmount it and use it as a miracle to move on to greater height."
— Ifeanyi Enoch Onuoha

299

"When in doubt, throw doubt out and have a little faith...."
— E.A. Bucchianeri

300

"One often has to do what they have to do in order to do what they want to do; however if you only do what you want to do then you will never do what you have to do!"
— C. Moorer

Motivational Quotes

301

"Do the best you can, with what you can, while you can, and success in inevitable."
— Steve Maraboli

302

"One should measure their life by the faith they embrace and the relationships they cherish"
— John Paul Warren

303

"You've got one life, one shot, and all the power to make it happen. Get ready to dream big and live big. It's all up to you. And it starts now."
— Jolene Stockman

Motivational Quotes

304

"Like love, like talent, like any other virtue, like anything else in this life, happiness needs to be nurtured - this is the truth of the whole matter."
— Ogwo David Emenike

305

"Changes are inevitable and not always controllable. What can be controlled is how you manage, react to and work through the change process."
— Kelly A. Morgan

306

"Be wise today so you don't cry tomorrow."
— E.A. Bucchianeri

307

"A barrier is a limitation only when you perceive it as one."
— Stephen Richards,

308

"I have learned that the harder you fall…the higher you bounce!"
— John Paul Warren

309

"A great dread fell on him, as if he was awaiting the pronouncement of some doom that he had long foreseen and vainly hoped might after all never be spoken. An overwhelming longing to rest and remain at peace by Bilbo's side in Rivendell filled all his heart. At last with an effort he spoke, and wondered to hear his own words, as if some other will was using his small voice.
"I will take the Ring," he said, "though I do not know the way."
— J.R.R. Tolkien

310

"Pain? Yes, of course. Racing without pain is not racing. But the pleasure of being ahead outweighed the pain a million times over. To hell with the pain. What's six minutes of pain compared to the pain they're going to feel for the next six months or six decades. You never forget your wins and losses in this sport. YOU NEVER FORGET."
— Brad Alan Lewis

311

"Forgive to forget, do not forget to forgive"
— Santosh Avvannavar,

312

"On the other hand, if the future is not the one you chose then you may have to use your willpower to obtain the future of your liking."
— Stephen Richards

313

"A story meant to motivate all and sundry
irrespective of their circumstances"
— Santosh Avvannavar

314

"I want every girl in the world to pick up a
guitar and start screaming."
— Courtney Love

315

"Most people know the physical senses, but a
lot of people don't know the soul's senses:
empathy, trust, intuition, love and harmony"
— Steven Aitchison

316

"If the world is a book, are you the hero, or just a walk-on part?"
— K.J. Parker

317

"If life throws you a few bad notes or vibrations, don't let them interrupt or alter your song."
— Suzy Kassem

318

"One thing I have learned from many years of watching my father is that some people, the best ones, are motivated more by the chance to prove themselves than by a command to serve. It is the work itself that calls them onward, especially if they believe they are the only ones who can do it."
— Rae Carson

Motivational Quotes

319

"When life's got you down, keep your head up... you can't see the ground anyway"
— Nicole Rae

320

"If you won't trust yourself, nobody else will."
— Anamika Mishra

321

"What if not just women, but both men and women, worked smart, more flexible schedules? What if the workplace itself was more fluid than the rigid and narrow ladder to success of the ideal worker? And what if both men and women became responsible for raising children and managing the home, sharing work, love, and play? Could everyone then live whole lives?"
— Brigid Schulte

322

"If you want your prayers answered, get up off your knees and do something about them."
— Wally Lamb

323

"Don't be distracted by criticism. Remember ~ the only taste of success some people have is when they take a bite out of you."
— Zig Ziglar

324

"What we perceive about ourselves is greatly a reflection of how we will end up living our lives."
— Stephen Richards

325

"Strength wasn't about being able to do everything alone. Strength was knowing when to ask for help and not being too proud to do it."
— Karen Marie Moning

326

"To become a master at any skill, it takes the total effort of your: heart, mind, and soul working together in tandem."
— Maurice Young

327

"What if I told you 10 years from now your life would be exactly the same?
Doubt you'd be happy.
So, why are you afraid of change?"
— Karen Salmansohn

Motivational Quotes

328

"Strength wasn't about being able to do everything alone. Strength was knowing when to ask for help and not being too proud to do it."
— Karen Marie Moning

329

"To become a master at any skill, it takes the total effort of your: heart, mind, and soul working together in tandem."
— Maurice Young

330

"What if I told you 10 years from now your life would be exactly the same?
Doubt you'd be happy.
So, why are you afraid of change?"
— Karen Salmansohn

331

"Yawns are not the only infectious things
out there besides germs.
Giggles can spread from person to person.
So can blushing.
But maybe the most powerful infectious
thing is the act of speaking the truth."
— Vera Nazarian

332

"Each person has got a voice inside them.
Communicate with it and take hold of it. Do
not let it push and shove you around – you are
its master!"
— Stephen Richards

333

"You're only responsible for yourself, Jess.
And that's the only person you can control.
Other people will either get it or they won't
but you can't define yourself by their
opinions."
— Susan Mallery

Motivational Quotes

334

"I may not be where I want to be, but if I stop now, I'll NEVER get where I'm going!"
— Laura Lynch

335

"Without adversity, there would be no growth, and without growth, there would be no lesson to be learned."
— Michelle Cruz-Rosado

336

"Nothing that happens to you was meant to be. The only thing about you that was meant to be is you. Blaze your own trail."
— George Alexiou

337

"There is no real world, just the one you create."
— Jolene Stockman

338

"Going down in history is a dead end pursuit"
— Benny Bellamacina

339

"All my life I've been fascinated by the precipice in all of us. When you come to it, you either choose to fall or you don't --Alvin Ailey"
— Kathy Petrakis

Motivational Quotes

340

"If your failure is not a lesson, it's indeed a failure."
— Ogwo David Emenike

341

"Therefore it is unnecessary for a prince to have all the good qualities I have enumerated, but it is very necessary to appear to have them. And I shall dare to say this also, that to have them and always to observe them is injurious, and that to appear to have them is useful; to appear merciful, faithful, humane, religious, upright, and to be so, but with a mind so framed that should you require not to be so, you may be able and know how to change to the opposite."
— Niccolò Machiavelli

342

"Someone needs to fight, someone needs to sacrifice, someone needs to inspire, someone needs to be a hero."
— Amit Kalantri

343

"Taking the decision-making process away from people disempowers them. It also makes them much less likely to buy into the decision, however right it may be. One's own conscience remains the ultimate arbiter."
— Lama Surya Das

344

"Then holding the star aloft and the bright sword advanced, Frodo, hobbit of the Shire, walked steadily down to meet the eyes."
— J.R.R. Tolkien,

345

"One of the Secrets in Life is to Make Stepping Stones out of Stumbling Blocks."
— Jack Penn

Motivational Quotes

346

"The power of hope! Even a lack of ambition can, for a time, pay off as a necessary facet, as long as hope outweighs it."
— Criss Jami

347

"I don't give up. That makes me incredibly resilient or maybe stupid or just plain stubborn. Whichever..."
— Destiny Booze

348

"Reconnect with the highest truth and ignite the divine sparks in you."
— Amit Ray

349

"The mind can't delete what the heart won't
let go of."
— Peggy Toney Horton

350

"For that reason, let a prince have the credit
of conquering and holding his state, the means
will always be considered honest, and he will
be praised by everybody because the vulgar
are always taken by what a thing seems to be
and by what comes of it; and in the world there
are only the vulgar, for the few find a place
there only when the many have no ground to
rest on."
— Niccolò Machiavelli

351

"If you can't be brave, be determined. And
you'll end up in the same place."
— Lisa Scottoline

352

"We often fail to see that there is an invisible wall in a relationship - Cord 10, In Between Us!"
— Santosh Avvannavar

353

"You spend your TIME to make a DIME. You lose your HEALTH to make your WEALTH, but at the end it is FUNNY because you leave back all your MONEY."
— R.v.m.

354

"Your only limitations are the ties you allow to bind you."
— Saundra Dalton-Smith

Motivational Quotes

355

"Never let the opinion of another affect your opinion of yourself."
— Teresa Mummert

356

"Encourage, lift and strengthen one another. For the positive energy spread to one will be felt by us all. For we are connected, one and all."
— Deborah Day

357

"Always strive to aim for the highest peak of the goals in life you have set, this way if you manage to reach even half way toward a goal, landing in the middle is not such a bad place to end up."
— Victoria Addino

Motivational Quotes

358

"What is done is done for the love of it- or not really done at all."
— Robert Frost

359

"Success is a decision, not a gift."
— Steve Backley

360

"Your environment will eat your goals and plans for breakfast."
— Steve Pavlina

361

"Pure happiness and peace are at their peak when your body is in harmony with itself."
— Asa Don Brown,

362

"Get out of your own way… stop the paralysis by analysis… decide what you want, create a simple plan, and get moving!"
— Steve Maraboli

363

"Gone are the days when 19-inch biceps would once command respect. A Jedi doesn't walk around with their arms flexed and with a thousand yard stare in their eyes. They walk with a good posture, their head held high and with a serious, yet friendly, look on their face."
— Stephen Richards

Motivational Quotes

364

"Nothing is permanent in my mysterious world, even my moments of belief - Jenifer"
— Durgesh Satpathy

365

"POEMINHA DO CONTRA
Todos estes que aí estão
Atravancando o meu caminho,
Eles passarão.
Eu passarinho!"
— Mario Quintana

366

"Every minute doing one thing is a minute not doing something else. Every choice is another choice not made another path grown over lost."
— Jerry Weintraub

Printed by Amazon Italia Logistica S.r.l.
Torrazza Piemonte (TO), Italy